My Amazing Body
SENSES

Angela Royston

www.raintreepublishers.co.uk
Visit our website to find out more information about **Raintree** books.

To order:
☎ Phone 44 (0) 1865 888112
▤ Send a fax to 44 (0) 1865 314091
▯ Visit the Raintree bookshop at **www.raintreepublishers.co.uk** to browse our catalogue and order online.

First published in Great Britain by Raintree, Halley Court, Jordan Hill, Oxford OX2 8EJ, part of Harcourt Education.
Raintree is a registered trademark of Harcourt Education Ltd.

Editorial: Nick Hunter and Catherine Clarke
Design: Kim Saar and Roslyn Broder
Illustrations: Will Hobbs, except p. 9: David Woodroffe and p. 15: Art Construction
Picture Research: Maria Joannou and Pete Morris
Production: Jonathan Smith

Originated by Dot Gradations Ltd
Printed and bound in China by South China Printing Company

ISBN 1 844 43387 0
08 07 06 05 04
10 9 8 7 6 5 4 3 2 1

British Library Cataloguing in Publication Data
Royston, Angela
Senses. - (My Amazing Body)
612.8
A full catalogue record for this book is available from the British Library.

Acknowledgements
The publishers would like to thank the following for permission to reproduce photographs:
Alamy Images p. **6**; Bubbles p. **28**; Corbis pp. **11**, **12**, **17**, **25**, **26** (Paul A. Souders); FLPA pp. **7**(Winfried Wisniewski), **24** (Silvestris Fotoservice); Gareth Boden p. **19**; Getty Images (Digital Vision) p. **13**; Pete Morris p. **4**; Photodisc p. **14**; Sally Greenhill pp. **23**, **27**; Science Photo Library pp. **5** (Scott Camazine), **8** (David Parker), **10** (Martin Dohrn), **16** (Susomo Nishinaga), **18** (Prof. P. Motta/G. Franchitto, University "La Sapienza", Rome), **21** (Tim Davis), **20** (Martin Dohrn).

Cover photograph of an MRI scan of the human brain, reproduced with permission of Science Photo Library (SOVEREIGN, ISM) and close-up of a human eye reproduced with permission of Science Photo Library (David Parker).

The publishers would like to thank Carol Ballard for her assistance in the preparation of this book.

Every effort has been made to contact copyright holders of any material reproduced in this book. Any omissions will be rectified in subsequent printings if notice is given to the publishers.

The paper used to print this book comes from sustainable resources.

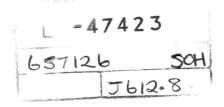

Contents

Inside and out 4

Why do I need my senses?....................6

Seeing..8

Blinking and crying.............................10

Wearing glasses.................................12

Hearing 14

Smelling......................................16

Tasting.......................................18

Touching......................................20

Feeling heat and cold 22

Itching and aching..............................24

What can go wrong? 26

The whole body.................................28

Find out for yourself...........................30

Glossary 31

Index...32

Any words appearing in bold, **like this**, are
explained in the Glossary.

Inside and out

Seeing, hearing, smelling, tasting and touching are called your senses. Each sense tells you something about the world around you, and some senses make you aware of things that happen inside your body.

How many senses do you think this girl is using while she eats this orange?

Sense organs

Each sense involves particular parts of the body. For example, you see with your eyes and hear with your ears. Your eyes, ears, nose, mouth and skin are called **sense organs** and they are on the outside of your body.

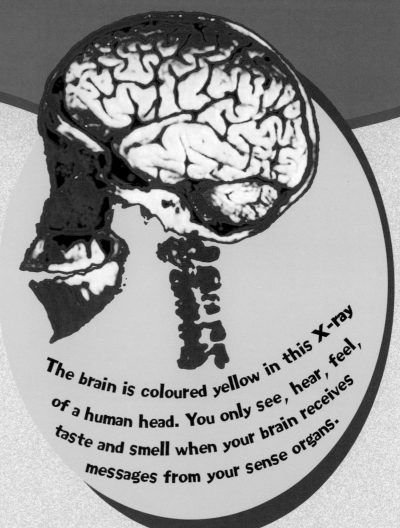

The brain is coloured yellow in this X-ray of a human head. You only see, hear, feel, taste and smell when your brain receives messages from your sense organs.

Messages to the brain

Each sense organ **reacts** to a certain thing. For example, your eyes react to light. When a sense organ reacts, it sends messages along nerves to your brain.

Animal senses

Many animals have keener senses than people. Most animals can hear sounds that people cannot. Bees can see colours that we cannot.

Why do I need my senses?

Without your senses, you would live in a dark and silent world. You would not be able to feel anything or know when something touched you. You would have no idea of where you were or what you needed.

Most important sense

Most people rely on their sense of sight more than any other sense. You use your eyes in almost everything you do – reading, watching television, walking along the road and even getting dressed.

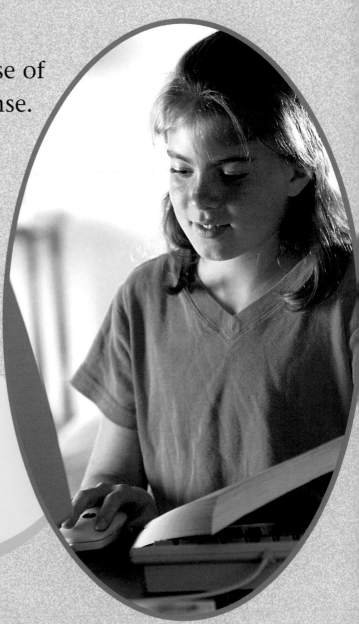

This girl is using her sense of sight to see her computer, and her sense of touch to work the mouse and hold a book at the same time!

Managing without sight

People who cannot see, rely on other senses. **Blind** people use their sense of touch to feel their way. They also listen more carefully to the sounds around them than **sighted** people do.

These animals may be attacked while they drink. They sniff, look and listen for danger.

Extra senses

Animals have the same kind of senses as people, but some animals have an extra sense that helps them to find their way. Some birds fly thousands of miles away when they **migrate**, but they always return to exactly the same place.

Seeing

You see when light enters your eyes. As light bounces off objects, we see their shapes and colours.

How light enters your eyes

In the centre of each eye is a round, black hole, called the pupil. Light goes through the pupil into your eye. The coloured circle around the pupil is a **muscle** called the iris.

The iris controls how much light can enter your eyes. The front of your eye is protected by a thin, clear covering.

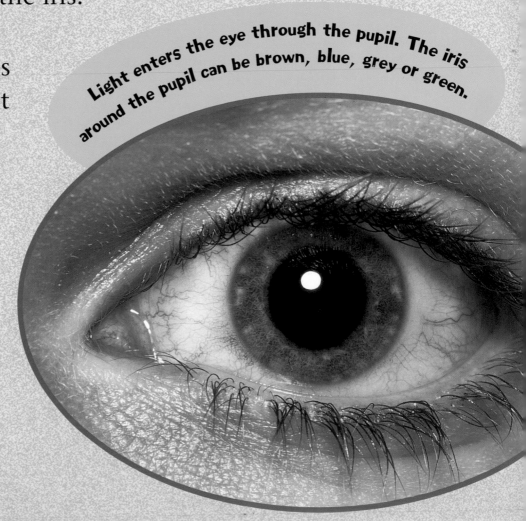

Light enters the eye through the pupil. The iris around the pupil can be brown, blue, grey or green.

Inside your eye

Behind your pupil is a **lens**. It makes sure that the light forms a clear pattern on your **retina** (back of your eye). Your retina contains **nerve** endings that send messages to your brain. Your brain uses these messages to form an ever-changing picture.

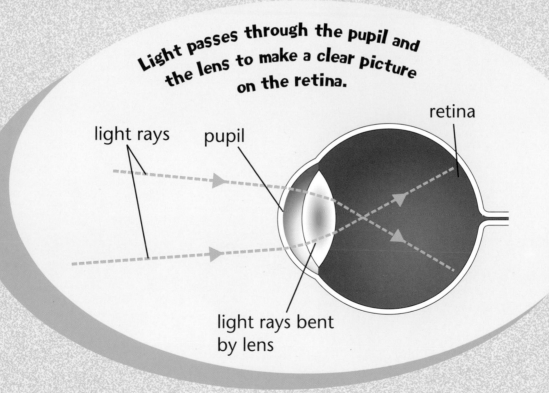

Light passes through the pupil and the lens to make a clear picture on the retina.

light rays

pupil

retina

light rays bent by lens

Eagle-eyed

Birds of **prey**, such as eagles and hawks, have extremely good eyesight. A kestrel in the air can spot a beetle moving more than 60 metres below it.

Blinking and crying

Your eyes are very **delicate**. Each eye is protected by an eyelid and a layer of salty water that covers the surface.

You close your eyes to shut out light and protect your eyes.

Blinking

You blink every few seconds. Every time you blink, you shut your eyes for an instant. Blinking spreads a fresh film of water across your eyeballs. This keeps them moist and helps to wipe away any dust or **germs** that have got into your eyes. You also blink when something touches your eyelashes or comes too close to your eyes.

Tears

If you do get something in your eye, your body makes extra water to wash it out. Normally, the water in your eyes drains into your nose, but this extra water often spills out of your eyes as tears.

Tears flow from our eyes when we are upset or when something irritates the surface of our eyes.

Unblinking stare

Snakes have no eyelids so they cannot blink or close their eyes. Instead, they have a hard see-through cover over their eyes.

Wearing glasses

Everyone should wear sunglasses to protect their eyes from the harmful rays of bright sunlight. Many people also wear other kinds of glasses to help them see better.

Lenses

Some people do not see clearly because the inside of their eyes do not work as well as they should. Instead of forming a clear picture on the **retina**, some things look blurred. Glasses bend the light to form a clear picture.

Direct sunlight can damage your eyes. Sunglasses protect your eyes, but you should NEVER look directly at the Sun, even when you are wearing sunglasses.

Lots of people need glasses to help them see more clearly.

People who are short-sighted can see only things that are close to them clearly. Their glasses make distant things look clear, too. Some people are long-sighted. They can see things that are far away, but not things that are close to them! They have to wear glasses to read or write.

Hearing

When something makes a sound, the air around it ripples with **sound waves**. The waves spread out and may reach your ears. Your ear changes the sound waves into messages that allow you to hear the sound.

Ear flaps

The ears on the side of your head are simply ear flaps. They collect sound and guide it into your ear. Many animals have ear flaps that are much better at collecting sound than ours are. Horses, antelope and rabbits all have large ear flaps on the top of their head. They can also turn their ears to hear even better.

Rabbits and hares use their huge ears to listen out for danger.

Inside an ear

Most of your ear is inside your head. Sounds pass into your ear through your eardrum. They then travel through three small bones and a spiral filled with **liquid** before they reach the **nerves** deep inside your ear.

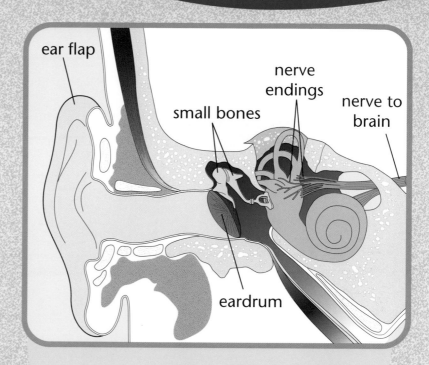

ear flap

nerve endings

small bones

nerve to brain

eardrum

Your eardrum is made of tight skin. Sounds pass through it into your ear. The nerves that react to sounds are deep inside your ears.

Bats

Some bats use their ears like radar to find their way in the dark. They make high-pitched squeaks that bounce back, or echo, off objects. Hearing the echoes tells the bats where things are.

Smelling

You can smell some things even though they are some way away from you. This is because tiny **particles**, which are too small to see, float into the air and reach your nose. **Nerve** endings in your nose **react** to the particles and send messages to your brain about the smell.

Inside your nose

The nerve endings that react to smells are right at the top of the inside of your nose. The more particles that reach your nose, the stronger the smell.

Tiny hairs in your nose trap dirt and dust from the air you breathe in. In this picture some of the hairs have been magnified many times and coloured yellow and orange.

To smell something better, you sniff. Sniffing draws in more air and pulls it higher up your nose to the nerve endings.

Telling smells apart

Some smells are pleasant and some are disgusting. No one knows how the nerve endings in your nose tell one smell from another, but your brain decides what smells you like and dislike.

Animal noses

Some dogs can smell so well they can track a person from the smell of their footprints. Dogs can smell much better than humans can because their whole nose is lined with nerve endings. Police train dogs to sniff out illegal **drugs**.

Tasting

To taste something, you lick it or swirl it around your mouth. If food tastes bad or rotten, you spit it out and don't swallow it. When food tastes good, though, you want to eat more of it.

Taste buds

You can taste because your tongue and mouth have taste buds containing **nerve** endings. When **particles** of food or **liquid** reach these nerve endings, they send messages to your brain about the taste.

This is what the surface of your tongue looks like, magnified by almost 200 times its real size! The yellow-orange area in the middle shows some taste buds.

Kinds of taste

Although you taste many different flavours, your taste buds sense only four main tastes – sweet, salty, sour and bitter. Every flavour is made up of a mixture of these main tastes. The tastes most people like best are salty and sweet. Lemons taste sour while pure chocolate tastes bitter. Chocolate is mixed with sugar to make it taste sweeter.

When you eat food like this Chinese meal, you can taste lots of different flavours.

Smell and taste

Your sense of taste relies on your sense of smell. When you have a cold and your nose is blocked, you cannot smell. Food becomes less tasty too.

Touching

You rely mainly on your skin to give you a sense of touch. **Nerve** endings in your skin send messages to your brain. Some nerve endings tell you what things feel like. Others tell you whether something is hot or cold, and others make you feel pain.

Sensitivity

Some parts of your skin are more **sensitive** than other parts. Your fingertips, the tip of your tongue, your lips and the soles of your feet are particularly sensitive to touch. This is because they contain more nerve endings than other parts of your body.

Your fingertips are sensitive to touch. The skin has ridges and contains many nerve endings that react to touch.

Using touch

You usually use your fingertips to tell you how something feels. It may feel rough or smooth, hard or soft. Your fingertips are so sensitive they can feel even tiny bumps.

A cat's fur feels soft and smooth and is nice to touch and stroke.

Cat's whiskers

A cat's whiskers are sensitive to touch. The cat uses them to feel its way in the dark. The whiskers are attached to nerves in the skin.

Feeling heat and cold

Different **nerves** in your skin **react** to heat and to cold. These nerves only react when something hot or cold touches your skin. You can feel the heat of a candle flame without touching it, because the flame heats the air around it, which touches your skin. Some parts of your body are more **sensitive** to heat and cold than other parts.

pain   cold   heat   light touch

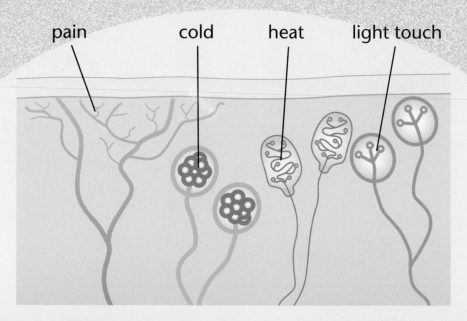

This diagram shows some of the different nerves in your skin that sense things like heat, cold and pain.

Lips and tongue

Your tongue and the inside of your mouth are easily burned by hot food or drinks. Because your lips are particularly sensitive to heat and cold, they check how hot something is before you put it in your mouth.

Testing bath water

Your feet are more sensitive to hot and cold than your hands are. Water may feel warm to your hand but too hot for your feet. Use your elbow, which is also sensitive to heat, to test how hot your bath water is.

This mother uses her elbow to test how hot her baby's bath water is.

Snakes

Some snakes use heat to find mice or other **prey** in the dark. Special nerve endings on the snake's head sense the heat from other animals' bodies.

Itching and aching

Different **nerves** in your skin **react** to different kinds of touch. Some nerves react to itching. Other nerves react to pain.

Itching

The surface of your skin is so **sensitive** you can feel even a light touch. When your skin itches, you usually scratch it until it stops itching. You should not scratch insect bites, **eczema** or chicken pox spots, however, because scratching them can damage the skin and they may become **infected**.

This dog is scratching an itch behind his ear. Animals feel itches and pain, just like humans do.

Pain

You feel pain when your skin is damaged, perhaps by heat or by being hit. Pain is important because it tells you that something is wrong. You also have nerves in other parts of your body to tell you about pain. You may sometimes get a stomach ache, for example, or a headache.

This boy is crying because he has fallen and hurt himself. If he did not feel pain, he might not realize that something was wrong.

Stopping pain

Some **drugs**, such as aspirin, help to lessen the feeling of pain. An anaesthetic is a drug that takes away your whole sense of touch, not just of pain.

What can go wrong?

Things can sometimes go wrong with the **nerves** and the **sense organs**. It does not matter too much if your sense of smell or taste does not work very well. If your eyes or ears don't work though, it affects the way you live.

This man cannot feel anything in his legs and feet because the nerves have been badly damaged, but it doesn't stop him from playing tennis.

Losing your sense of touch

When you have been kneeling for a long time, your legs may go numb. This is because you have squashed the nerves in the skin. The nerves quickly recover, but tingle uncomfortably as they do so. If you have an accident that damages the nerves in your spine, they may not recover. This means you would be unable to feel anything in part of your body.

Blindness and deafness

Most **blind** people can see some light and dark, but not enough to tell what things are.

People are deaf when their ears do not work properly. Some deaf people are able to understand what people are saying by watching the shapes their lips make as they speak.

This blind woman is using a stick to feel the ground in front of her.

Colour blind

People are colour blind when they cannot tell all the different colours apart. Many animals, including cats, are colour blind. They see most colours as shades of grey.

The whole body

You could do almost nothing without your senses. You could perhaps lie still and breathe, but eating would be difficult if you could not feel the food in your mouth.

Moving around

You use your **muscles** and bones to move your body, but you would not know where to move without your senses. You have to be able to feel something to pick it up – and you need your sense of touch to know when it is in your hand.

These children are enjoying themselves on a bouncy castle! They are using their eyes and ears, as well as their muscles and brains.

Using your brain

All the information collected by your senses is sent to your brain. Your brain uses it to decide what to do.

When someone throws you a ball, for example, you use your eyes to track its path and to put your hands in the right place to catch it. It would be very difficult for people and animals to survive without their senses.

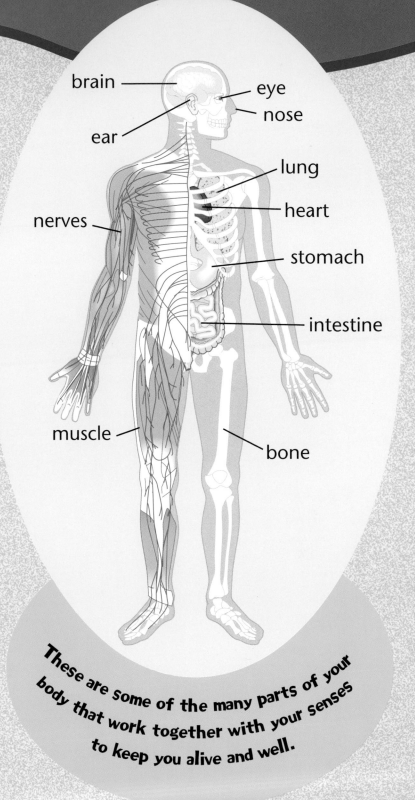

brain — eye — nose — ear — lung — heart — nerves — stomach — intestine — muscle — bone

These are some of the many parts of your body that work together with your senses to keep you alive and well.

Find out for yourself

Everybody's body is slightly different but they all work in the same way. Find out more about how your own amazing body works by noticing what happens to it. When you are blindfolded, can you tell what different tastes are? How well can you see in the dark? Does water feel hotter to your feet or to your hand? You will find the answers to many of your questions in this book, but you can also use other books and the Internet.

Books to read

Why do I get Toothache? And other questions about nerves, Angela Royston (Heinemann Library, 2002)

How our bodies work: Feel and Touch, Taste and Smell, Carol Ballard (Hodder Wayland, 2001)

Look at your body: Brain and Nerves, Steve Parker (Franklin Watts, 2001)

Using the Internet

Explore the Internet to find out more about your senses. Websites can change, but if some of the links below no longer work, don't worry. Use a search engine, such as www.yahooligans.com or www.internet4kids.com and type in keywords such as 'senses', 'seeing' and 'hearing'.

Websites:

www.kidshealth.org contains lots of information about how your body works and how to stay healthy

www.bbc.co.uk/science/humanbody/body contains an interactive body and lots of information. Click on brain to find out more about how your brain works.

www.brainpop.com click on 'health' for quizzes and films about different parts of the body, including your senses.

Disclaimer

All the Internet addresses (URLs) given in this book were valid at the time of going to press. However, due to the dynamic nature of the Internet, some addresses may have changed, or sites may have ceased to exist since publication. While the author and publishers regret any inconvenience this may cause readers, no responsibility for any such changes can be accepted by either the author or the publishers.

Glossary

blind unable to see

delicate easily damaged

drug chemical that affects the body or brain. Medical drugs are used to treat illnesses. Harmful drugs that can damage the body are illegal.

eczema condition that makes patches of skin dry and itchy

germ tiny form of life that can make you ill. Germs are so small that you need a microscope to see them.

infect bring in germs

lens curved piece of glass or other see-through material that changes the direction of rays of light

liquid flowing substance that is not a gas or a solid. Water is a liquid.

microscope instrument that makes very tiny things look large enough to see

migrate move to a warmer place for part of the year

muscle part of the body that you use to move your bones

nerve fibre that carries messages from the sense organs to the brain. Another kind of nerve carries messages from the brain to the muscles.

particle very tiny piece of something

prey animal that is caught and eaten by another animal

react respond to

retina back of the eye

sense organ part of the body that reacts to either light, sound, chemicals or touch to produce one of the senses

sensitive easily affected

sighted able to see

sound wave movements in the air that your ears respond to, to hear sounds

X-ray kind of photograph that shows parts of the inside of your body, such as your bones or brain

Index

anaesthetics 25
animals 5, 7, 9, 11, 14, 15, 17, 21, 23, 24, 27

bats 15
bees 5
birds 7, 9
blind people 7, 27
blinking 10
brain 5, 9, 16, 17, 18, 29

cats 21, 27
colour blindness 27

deaf people 27
dogs 17, 24
drugs 17, 25

eardrum 15
ears 5, 14–15, 26, 27
eyes 5, 6, 8–13, 26, 29

feet 20, 23
fingertips 20, 21

glasses 12–13

hearing 4, 5, 14–15, 27
heat and cold 20, 22, 23

itching 24

lenses 9, 12
lips 23

migration 7
mouth and tongue 5, 18, 23

nerves 5, 9, 15, 16, 17, 18, 20, 22, 24, 25, 26
nose 5, 16, 17, 19

pain 20, 24, 25

retina 9, 12

seeing 4, 5, 6, 8–13, 27, 29
sense organs 5, 26
skin 5, 20, 22, 24, 25
smelling 4, 5, 16–17, 19, 26
snakes 11, 23
sniffing 17
sound waves 14
sunlight 12

taste buds 18, 19
tasting 4, 5, 18–19, 26
tears 11
touching 4, 5, 6, 7, 20–25, 26, 28

whole body 28–29

Raintree Perspectives version

Titles in the *My Amazing Body* series include:

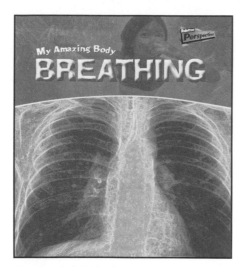

Hardback 1 844 43383 8

Hardback 1 844 43384 6

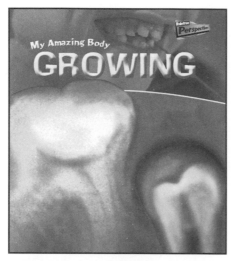

Hardback 1 844 43385 4

Hardback 1 844 43386 2

Hardback 1 844 43387 0

Hardback 1 844 43388 9

Find out about the other titles in this series on our website www.raintreepublishers.co.uk